rock'n'roll

danceclub

rock'n'roll

paul bottomer

southwater

This edition is published by Southwater

Southwater is an imprint of Anness Publishing Ltd
Hermes House, 88–89 Blackfriars Road, London SE1 8HA
tel. 020 7401 2077; fax 020 7633 9499
info@anness.com

© Anness Publishing Ltd 1996, 2002

Published in the USA by Southwater,
Anness Publishing Inc
fax 212 807 6813

This edition distributed in the UK by
The Manning Partnership
tel. 01225 852 727; fax 01225 852 852

This edition distributed in the USA
by National Book Network
tel. 301 459 3366; fax 301 459 1705

This edition distributed in Canada by
General Publishing
tel. 416 445 3333; fax 416 445 5991

This edition distributed in Australia by
Sandstone Publishing
tel. 02 9560 7888; fax 02 9560 7488

This edition distributed in New Zealand by
The Five Mile Press (NZ) Ltd
tel. (09) 444 4144; fax (09) 444 4518

A CIP catalogue record for this book is available from the British Library.

1 3 5 7 9 10 8 6 4 2

Publisher: Joanna Lorenz
Senior Editor: Lindsay Porter
Photographer: Anthony Pickhaver
Make-up: Bettina Graham
Designer: Siân Keogh

Previously published as *Dance Crazy Rock'n'Roll*

Contents

Introduction

Dance styles have always followed musical trends and none more so than the dance which was to become Rock 'n' Roll. While we tend to think of the Rock 'n' Roll phenomenon as beginning in the fifties, the dance actually started emerging more than two decades earlier in the USA. During the early twenties, there had been a veritable zoo of animal dances, the best known of which was probably the Turkey Trot. These were in addition to other dance crazes, such as the Charleston and Black Bottom, whose wild moves got wilder as the music got faster. Other dances and styles developed from these and the Texas Tommy or Breakaway, in which the couple moved apart and came back together, emerged during the twenties among the black population of America.

By the end of the decade, this style was extremely popular. In 1927, when Charles Lindbergh piloted the Spirit of St Louis solo across the Atlantic, the newspaper headlines declaring this event were adopted as the new name for the dance, the Lindy Hop. As the dance continued to develop into the thirties, it found a home in the Harlem Savoy Ballroom, where it grew up with the great Swing bands of the era. The line-up of orchestras who played there sounds like a Who's Who of Swing. Benny Goodman, Cab Calloway, Tommy Dorsey, Louis Armstrong, Count Basie and Duke Ellington all performed at the Savoy. The bands inspired the dancers and the dancers inspired the bands in an upward-reaching spiral towards new heights of dance and musical expression. When Benny Goodman gave a concert at the Paramount Theatre, New York, in 1937, teenagers went wild and poured into the aisles to "Jitterbug", as the newspapers called the dance. The craze

Left: The spirit of fifties Rock 'n' Roll is as popular as ever in specialist clubs and classes.

swept across America. Variations in technique led to styles such as Boogie-woogie and Swing Boogie, with "Jive" gradually emerging as the generic term that covered the family of Lindy Hop, Jitterbug and Boogie-woogie dances. Whichever term was used to in the forties, the music was always Swing.

After the Second World War, bands got smaller and the music changed. By the fifties, the music was no longer as smooth and polished as swing but it had huge popular appeal; this music was Rock 'n' Roll. With the change in musical style came a change in the dancers' interpretation of the music. The heavier beat engendered a more two-dimensional jive with a "choppier" feel. By the end of the fifties, jive had already reached the ballrooms and dance schools but in a different style.

The basis of all the dances from the Lindy Hop, through Boogie-woogie to Rock 'n' Roll is virtually the same: a six-beat musical rhythm (though the Lindy Hop also used an eight-beat rhythm). In the basic dance, the dancers take two steps which rock or swing sideways, then a step backwards and a replace step. The step backwards and replace movement remained fairly standard, as it gave the dances their rhythmic point of reference. However, the sideways rock or swing steps underwent many changes of style.

In Boogie-woogie, a tap is often added to make the sequence: tap, step, tap, step, step back, replace. The steps are danced well down into the knees.

In Rock 'n' Roll competitions, the Boogie taps became flicks in the sequence: flick, step, flick, step, step back, replace. This style has become quite extreme in Rock 'n' Roll dance competitions, with routines of dazzling acrobatic moves interspersed with the more basic dance moves. While it is very impressive, this performance style owes more to acrobatic prowess than to the notion of a man and woman coming together to dance. Most dancers prefer to dance to good music for their own enjoyment, which is the focus of this book, leaving the performance hybrid of Rock 'n' Roll to others.

The figures or moves introduced in this book are described without flicks or taps. When you have practised and are confident with the basic steps, you can add the Rock 'n' Roll flicks or the Boogie taps if you prefer. Rock 'n' Roll is danced more upright because of the flicking action, while the Boogie style calls for very flexed knees.

Right: Rock 'n' Roll is more about attitude than technique.

7

Music becomes popular when it reflects the mood of the people or the mood to which they aspire at the time it appears. The innovators of the musical style become role models and musicians become popular by creating the backdrop. People become a part of the process by getting onto the floor and expressing themselves as they dance. In contrast to the dance school Jive, which could look relatively formal, Rock 'n' Roll had a raw, unrefined quality with a hint of rebellion that appealed to young people. Jens Kressler, one of the top authorities on Boogie-woogie in Germany, invites his students to "look ugly" when they dance. Of course,

they don't really look ugly, he is merely empowering and encouraging them to "let go" and forget about a formal style. This idea of dancing how you feel to the music is what Rock 'n' Roll is all about.

So, what is the point of learning a technique? Many original Rock 'n' Rollers of the fifties often say that they did not learn a technique, but simply watched and danced the moves they had seen. Of course, when they watched other dancers, they were learning a technique but in an informal way. Although some Rock 'n' Rollers are proud of the fact that they have had no "training", you will often find that the man and woman are dancing independently of each other with no common rhythm or structure. If they are enjoying themselves, this is fine, but they will never be able to add new standard moves to their dance, which is a pity.

When a man and a woman come together to dance with each other, there must be some framework within which to operate or the result will be, at best, continuous improvisation, which is unsatisfying, and, at worst, complete chaos. Learning a technique provides the guidelines and a basis of common understanding on which a couple can build their dance together. The technique becomes particularly helpful when dancing with a new partner. If you both share the basic technique and don't immediately try launching into the more advanced figures until you know one another's capabilities, you can enjoy Rockin' 'n' Rollin' together.

Left: Fifties music captured the popular imagination, and paved the way for the development of earlier dances into the Rock 'n' Roll style.

What to Wear

At a few, very specialist Rock 'n' Roll clubs and special events, Teddy Boy outfits may still prevail. The Teddy Boys adopted their own version of the American zoot suit and were called "Teddy Boys" because the long, knee-length drape coats were reminiscent of Edwardian coats. Teddy Boys, or "Teds", often wore thick-soled shoes known as "beetle crushers", tight, leg-hugging "drain pipe" trousers and a "lace" tie or at least a narrow tie to complete the outfit. Hair was creamed and manipulated to extend in front in a "quiff" and rolled at the back into a "D.A.", so-called because it stuck up, resembling a duck's tail feathers. Girls wore dresses with full skirts, often with a bright floral design and sometimes with petticoats to fill out the skirt. Low-heeled shoes or pumps were worn.

At most clubs, the style of dress is far more casual. On your first visit, it is advisable to dress down to give yourself the chance to see what others are wearing. You could also call the club first to ask for advice. Ultimately, the most important thing is to wear what you feel comfortable in. There are a few rules though: avoid trainers, which will severely inhibit your ability to turn – and no-one appreciates a squeaky Rock 'n' Roller. Trainers can also become heavy very quickly and make the feet hot and prone to swelling. Any light shoes are fine and dance shoes with a silvered suede sole give a good grip and allow you to feel the floor. They are available in a wide variety of styles, finishes and colours and, if you are planning to dance regularly, are well worth the modest investment. Avoid shiny black patent leather shoes: they are specifically for standard (ballroom) dancing and the patent finish causes the shoes to stick together when they come into contact. Jazz shoes are too specialized a product to be stocked by most general shoe shops, and can be found in dance shoe outlets. Consult your telephone directory or call a local dance school if you have problems finding dance shoes. Most dance teachers sell shoes and may be able to help.

Getting Started

Initially, the most important thing is to get to grips with the rhythm. This is vital because, even when you and your partner know the moves, you will have to synchronize with each other to make the steps work and your cue is the rhythm. First, listen to some Rock 'n' Roll tracks. Rock 'n' Roll music has four beats to each bar of music. To start with, listen to the drum or rhythm line rather than to the melody. The drum provides the beat and you will notice that the drummer emphasizes beats 1 and 3 in each bar. You do not need to understand musical bars, just to be able to hear the all-important beat. A "quick" count equals one beat of music, while a "slow" count equals two beats. In a few figures, such as the Arm Breaker or the Full Catapult, two steps are danced to one beat of music. These are indicated by an "&" count, and are danced "quick, and" in the space of one beat. In the steps for each figure, the rhythm is shown in parentheses.

The man and woman's roles in Rock 'n' Roll are quite clearly defined. The man's job is generally to stay put, while the woman moves more around the floor. The roles of each can be summted up as follows:

The man's main role:
• To keep the couple synchronized with the music and with each other. The woman must synchronize with the man, even if he is off-time with the music. This role is particularly important as an aid to the woman when she has completed a spin or turn and needs a point of reference to continue the dance in time with the music.

• To decide which figures to dance and in which order, leading the woman to dance them. Your main responsibility is to make your own moves clear and decisive to avoid confusing your partner. The lead should be clear and firm rather than strong and aggressive. The idea is to communicate the move to the woman rather than force her to dance it.

• To provide a point of orientation for the woman. While you stay mainly in place and the woman dances towards, around and away from you, it is easy for her to become disorientated. On completion of each move, she will be looking to orientate herself on your position before starting the next move. The man's steps are generally less difficult than the woman's, allowing you to "manage" the dance.

The woman's main role:
• To be aware of the man's intentions as communicated by his lead and not to anticipate or guess moves. If you anticipate a move by committing your body weight in a certain direction too early, the man will have to revise his intentions, although he is in the worst position to do so. The resulting moves can be very clumsy.

• To check constantly that your rhythm is synchronized with that of the man and that you are orientating yourself in relation to him, particularly as a move ends. Check your rhythm on each "back, replace" step. If you are not synchronized with the man, don't try to slow down or speed up your next move to compensate. Just stop briefly and start again.

Couples should keep themselves from getting carried away by the music at the cost of getting the steps and rhythm wrong. More concentration is required in the learning stage but it will be amply rewarded when swinging from one figure to another becomes second nature to you. On the "back, replace" step, you should mostly be opposite your partner or sometimes side by side. Whichever it is, make sure that you are clearly in this position. If you are not and your partner decides to continue with a move requiring a strong lead, you may find your own body weight and impetus working against you, which can sometimes result in injuries such as a sprained wrist or jarred shoulder. Rock 'n' Roll is not in itself a dangerous dance but common sense should prevail.

THE BASIC HOLD

There are a number of holds in Rock 'n' Roll dancing. The hold will depend on the preceding move, the current move and the following move. The transition from one type of hold to another should be quite natural. Tips on how to achieve this are given in the text as each change of hold is required.

To start the dance, face your partner with your feet slightly apart. The man stands with his weight on the right foot and the woman with her weight on the left foot. The man slips his right hand around the woman's waist, without drawing her too close to him. The woman rests her left hand comfortably on the man's upper right arm. Her right hand is held in the man's left hand, palm to palm and with her fingers between his fingers and thumb, her thumb curled around his thumb.

Left: Use the basic hold to start off the dance, although you may use other holds as the dance progresses.

11

Rock Basic

In this introduction to Rock 'n' Roll, the descriptions of the figures or moves will use the basic steps without flicks or taps. Later, when you have practised, you can add the Rock 'n' Roll flicks or the Boogie taps as preferred. In this basic move, is essential that the knees remain quite flexed. Steps 3 and 4 are known as the "back, replace" steps and will be referred to often in the book.

1 Man
Rock to the side onto the left foot, taking a small step and leaving the right foot in place. (Count - slow)

Woman
Rock to the side onto the right foot, taking a small step and leaving the left foot in place. (Count - slow)

2 Man
Rock to the side onto the right foot, taking a small step and leaving the left foot in place. (Count - slow)

Woman
Rock to the side onto the left foot, taking a small step and leaving the right foot in place. (Count - slow)

3 Man
Rock onto the left foot, moving it under the body and placing the left toe behind the right heel. Lift the right foot just off the floor. (Count - quick)

Woman
Rock onto the right foot, moving it under the body and placing the right toe behind the left heel. Lift the left foot just off the floor. (Count - quick)

12

Style Tips

On Steps 1 and 2, you might like to sway a little in the direction of the step to improve the feeling. (For the man, this will also give a nice indication to the woman to move.) Do not use heels on any steps.

Try to keep the feet under the body during the moves to avoid creating excessive movement and making the dance difficult. Small steps are far more controlled than large ones.

LINK

Many Rock 'n' Roll figures end with the woman facing the man in what is described as an "open hold". This is where the couple are holding only one hand, generally the woman's right hand in either of the man's hands, and are standing roughly one arm's length apart. This really is only one arm's length, as both partners' arms should be flexed. When you finish a move in the open hold, you can resume the Rock Basic by dancing the Link. This is very similar to the Rock Basic, except that Steps 1 and 2 are used by the man to draw the couple together again.

4 Man
Transfer your body weight forward onto the right foot.
(Count - quick)

Woman
Transfer your body weight forward onto the left foot.
(Count - quick)

Repeat the Rock Basic as many times as you want as a useful way of practising dancing to the rhythm. The Rock Basic can also be turned gently in an anticlockwise direction during Steps 1 and 2. At least four Rock Basics should be used to turn a full circle.

Throwaway

Experienced Rock 'n' Rollers will not use a set program or routine, but before you get to that stage, it is useful to put together a practice program. The Throwaway can be introduced immediately after the Rock Basic. The man dances the Rock Basic, turning on Steps 1 and 2 and leading the woman into an open position. Steps 3 and 4 remain the same.

1 Man

Rock to the side onto the left foot, taking a small step and starting to turn to the left. Lead the woman to start to turn by bringing your left hand down to the left hip.
(Count - slow)

Woman

Rock forward onto the right foot, toward the man's left side.
(Count - slow)

2 Man

Rock to the side onto the right foot, taking a small step and completing the quarter turn to the left. Lead the woman into an open position by moving your left hand forward at waist height. (Count - slow)

Woman

Turn on the right foot to face the man and rock backward onto the left foot away from the man into an open position. (Count - slow)

3–4 Man

Dance Steps 3 and 4 of the Rock Basic (the back, replace steps).
(Counts - quick, quick)

Woman

Dance Steps 3 and 4 of the Rock Basic. (Counts - quick, quick)

14

Underarm Turn to the Right

This very popular figure features a turn to the right. The couple have danced the by now familiar rhythm of the Rock Basic and have just finished the back, replace steps. They are standing in an open position with a left hand to right hand hold. The man is standing on the right foot and the woman on the left foot.

1 Man

Rock to the side onto the left foot, lifting the left arm to lead the woman to turn underneath. (Count - slow)

Woman

Turn underneath the man's left arm. Rock forward onto the right foot, starting to turn to the right. (Count - slow)

2 Man

Rock to the side onto the right foot, making a quarter turn to the left and returning the left hand to waist height. (Count - slow)

Woman

Rock to the side and back onto the left foot, continuing to turn to the right underneath the man's arm. (Count - slow)

3–4 Man

Dance Steps 3 and 4 of the Rock Basic. (Counts - quick, quick)

Woman

Dance Steps 3 and 4 of the Rock Basic continuing the turn to end facing the man. (Counts - quick, quick)

Practice Programme

You can now continue with a Link and the Rock Basic. The programme can be danced in the sequence: Rock Basic (dance several times, including a rotation to the left, if desired), Throwaway, Underarm Turn to the Right, Link, Rock Basic.

15

American or Push Spin

After a little more practice, you will now be ready to learn your first spin. A spin is no more than a turn which is made on one foot, as opposed to a turn, where two or more steps are taken. The man can lead the spin with either hand and he can resume hold after the spin with either hand. Here, we will pick up from the Underarm Turn to the Right, so the man is holding the woman's right hand in his left hand. The couple have just completed the back, replace steps. The man is now standing on the right foot and the woman is facing him, standing on the left foot.

1 Man

Rock forward onto the left foot, taking a slightly larger step than usual. Draw the woman towards you, bringing the left elbow firmly to the left hip. (Count - slow)

Woman

Relax and keep the knees flexed throughout the figure. Rock forward onto the right foot, moving towards the man's right side. Keep the right arm toned and lean into the step. (Count - slow)

2 Man

Release hold with the left hand and rock to the side onto the right foot. (Count - slow)

Woman

Still standing on the right foot, make a three-quarter turn to the right, if necessary pushing off the man's left arm and releasing hold with the right hand. Rock to the side onto the left foot. (Count - slow)

The right hand to right hand hold is taken up in preparation for the next move. However, if you prefer to incorporate the American or Push Spin in your practice programme, resume a man's left hand to woman's right hand hold and dance a Link.

3–4 Man

Dance the usual back, replace steps, resuming a right hand to right hand hold on Step 4. (Counts - quick, quick)

Woman

Dance the usual back, replace steps, completing the turn to face the man and resuming a right hand to right hand hold. (Counts - quick, quick)

Leading the American or Push Spin with the Right Hand

During the Underarm Turn to the Right, the man can quite easily change hold by taking the woman's right hand and placing it into his right hand at the end of Step 2 of the turn. At the end of the figure, the man can then lead the American Spin with the right hand in exactly the same way as when using the left hand. The woman will now move towards the man's right hip rather than his left hip, but otherwise the spin is the same.

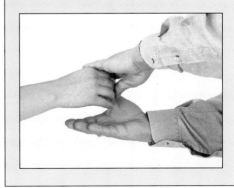

Comb

This figure has come to typify the Rock 'n' Roll style, despite the fact that it was already used 20 years before the Rock 'n' Roll era in the Lindy Hop. Teddy Boys were renowned for the care they took over their hair which involved frequent combing, hence the name of this classic figure. As usual, the couple have danced the back, replace steps. The man is now standing on the right foot and the woman on the left foot. The couple are in a right hand to right hand hold ready to dance the Comb.

1 Man
Rock to the side onto the left foot towards the woman, lifting the right hands over your head as if combing your hair…
Woman
Rock forward onto the right foot towards the man, allowing him to raise your right hand over his head…

1 (continued) **Man**
…End with the right hand at your right shoulder. (Count - slow)
Woman
…It is comfortable to turn slightly to the left to a side-by-side position. (Count - slow)

3–4 Man

Dance the usual back, replace steps, resuming an open facing position. (Counts - quick, quick)

Woman

Dance the usual back, replace steps, resuming an open facing position. End standing on the left foot. (Counts - quick, quick)

2 Man

Rock to the side onto the right foot away from the woman, releasing the right hand and allowing the woman's right hand to slip down your arm to your left hand, where you resume hold. (Count - slow)

Woman

Rock backwards onto the left foot, sliding the right hand down the man's left arm to resume hand hold. (Count - slow)

Style Tip

It is typical of fifties-style Rock 'n' Roll for the man to lean back a little on Steps 1 and 2 of this and, indeed, many of the figures.

When practising, follow the Comb with a Link and resume your practice programme. If you want to start exploring other options, try following the Comb with the Underarm Turn to the Right and perhaps an American Spin led with the right hand.

Double Spin

So far, the man has been dancing little more than the Rock Basic, adapting it to suit the moves and turns of the woman. Now it's time for the man to get a slice of the action and to jazz up the American Spin at the same time. The name of the figure does not mean spinning twice, merely that the man joins the woman and performs his own spin. To make this work, both the man and the woman must stay cool and try not to overdo it. Flex the knees during the spin to aid balance and maintain a controlled action.

1 Man

Rock forward onto the left foot, taking a slightly larger step than usual. Lean into the step slightly and draw the woman towards you, bringing your left elbow firmly to your left hip with the left arm parallel to the floor. You should feel the woman leaning into your left arm.
(Count - slow)

Woman

Dance Steps 1–4 of the American Spin as before. (Counts - slow, slow, quick, quick)

2 Man

Release hold and, standing on the left foot, make a three-quarter turn to the left. Rock to the side onto the right foot and resume hand hold. (Count - slow)

MUSIC SUGGESTION

"Cincinatti Fireball" by Johnny Burnette (Liberty Records), is a steady number, and a good one to start with as you build up your practice programme

3–4 Man

Dance the back, replace steps as usual, continuing to turn to the left to end facing your partner. (Counts - quick, quick)

Half Catapult

Just as you are recovering from the Double Spin, it's time to try another great Rock 'n' Roll move. Start in a right hand to right hand hold in an open position. To get into this position, you could dance an Underarm Turn to the Right with a hand change at the end, an American Spin ending right hand to right hand or a Double Spin. You will have completed the figure with the usual back, replace steps.

1 Man
Rock to the side onto the left foot, leading the woman forward towards your right side. (Count - slow)

Woman
Rock forward onto the right foot, towards the left of the man's position but not too close to the man and making sure you leave yourself enough space to turn into. (Count - slow)

2 Man

Rock to the side onto the right foot, leading the woman to turn to her right on the spot by moving your right arm forward but not across. (Count - slow)

Woman

Rock onto the left foot, leaving the right foot in place. Standing on the right foot, swivel a half turn to the right to end in a side-by-side position. It is comfortable to rest your left hand on the man's right shoulder. (Count - slow)

3–4 Man

Dance the back, replace steps in a side-by-side position. (Counts - quick, quick)

Woman

Dance the back, replace steps in a side-by-side position. (Counts - quick, quick)

6 Man

Rock onto the right foot, lowering the right hand behind the woman's head to lead her to turn right. (Count - slow)

Woman

Standing on the right foot, swivel a complete turn to the right and rock to the side onto the left foot. (Count - slow)

5 Man

Rock onto the left foot, making a quarter turn to the right to face the woman. Draw the woman towards you by raising the right hand. (Count - slow)

Woman

Rock to the side onto the right foot, making a quarter turn to the left. (Count - slow)

7–8 Man

Dance the back, replace steps
to end in an open position.
(Counts - quick, quick)

Woman

Dance the back, replace steps
facing the man. (Counts -
quick, quick)

Style Tip

As the arm lowers on Step 6, the man
may choose to resume practising
your programme by using a Link. If
you are feeling more confident, remain
in a right hand to right hand hold and
make a quarter turn on Steps 7 and 8,
to the left for the man and to the right
for the woman. You will end in a side-
by-side position, ready to move
straight into the next figure.

Jig Walks

This classy figure has its origins in the wild moves of the Lindy Hop, rather than the popular Gallic dance its name might imply. It is equally at home in Boogie-woogie and Rock 'n' Roll and can look quite stunning. However, most dancers learn very quickly how to dance it properly and avoid damage during the simultaneous kicking between their partners' legs. The figure can be preceded by something as simple as the Rock Basic, but this probably won't give a clear indication to the woman of what is to follow. It is more appropriate for less experienced dancers to "plan" the Jig Walks into their programme and a great place to insert them is immediately after the Half Catapult has ended in the side-by-side position. Turn on the replace movement of the back, replace steps to a close facing position.

1 Man

Holding the woman quite close to you, lift the left knee and kick the left foot out and downwards, keeping the foot loose. Your left leg will be above the woman's right leg during the kick. (Count - quick)

Woman

The man's adoption of a close hold indicates that you will be dancing the Jig Walks. Lift the right knee and kick the right foot out and downwards, keeping the foot loose. Your right leg will be below the man's left leg during the kick. (Count - quick)

2 Man
Step onto the left foot.
(Count - quick)
Woman
Step onto the right
foot. (Count - quick)

3 Man
Lift the right knee
and kick the right
foot out…
Woman
Lift the left knee
and kick the left
foot out…

MUSIC SUGGESTION

"Shake, Rattle and Roll" and "See You Later Alligator" by Bill Haley and his Comets (MCA) are two Rock 'n' Roll classics with steady tempos that are great for practice.

3 (continued) Man
… and downward,
keeping the foot loose.
Your right leg will be
below the woman's left
leg during the kick.
(Count - quick)
Woman
… and downward,
keeping the foot loose.
Your left leg will be
above the man's right
leg during the kick.
(Count - quick)

4 Man

Step onto the right foot. (Count - quick) Retention of the close hold will communicate to the woman that you will continue with another four counts of Jig Walks. Otherwise, continue clearly into the basic back, replace steps.

Woman

Step onto the right foot. (Count - quick)

Once you have practised this figure, you can enjoy dancing multiple Jig Walks, rotating them on the spot in a clockwise direction. To continue into your programme after the back, replace steps, simply dance a Rock Basic.

The Kicks

It should be common sense not to raise the knee high nor to make the kicks high. Many newcomers to this figure nervously hold back, believing that to get in close to their partner increases the likelihood of injury. In reality, the opposite is true, so move as close in to your partner as possible before starting the kicks. Try to use a little bounce action in the standing knee, as this communicates the rhythm of the kicks and weight transfers to your partner and avoids a stilted action, which would destroy the pleasure of this terrific figure.

Basic Turns

It is practical to intersperse basic turns between figures. There are a variety of turns which can be danced from either the basic hold or the open position.

CHANGE OF PLACE RIGHT TO LEFT

To dance the Change of Place Right to Left, start in the basic hold. Dance a Rock Basic and finish with the man on the right foot and the woman on the left foot, ready to go into this turn.

1 Man
Rock to the side onto the left foot, raising the left arm to lead the woman to dance under your arm to the right. It is sometimes helpful to use the right hand to confirm to the woman that she is about to dance under your arm.
(Count - slow)

Woman
Rock forward onto the right foot, starting to turn to the right.
(Count - slow)

2 Man
Rock to the side onto the right foot, making a quarter turn to the left. End by lowering the left arm to waist height.
(Count - slow)

Woman
Turning to the right under the man's arm, rock backwards onto the left foot to face the man. (Count - slow)

Dance the back, replace steps, then continue with the Underarm Turn to the Right or dance the next figure.

CHANGE OF PLACE LEFT TO RIGHT

This figure retraces the path of the Change of Place Right to Left.

1 Man

Rock to the side onto the left foot, raising the left arm to lead the woman across to your right. (Count - slow)

Woman

Rock forward onto the right foot, moving towards your left of the man. (Count - slow)

2 Man

Rock to the side onto the right foot, making a quarter turn to the right. End by lowering the left arm to a basic hold. (Countt - slow)

Woman

Standing on the right foot, turn left under the man's arm to face him and rock to the side onto the left foot. (Count - slow)

3–4 Man

Dance the back, replace steps, facing the woman in a basic hold. (Counts - quick, quick)

Woman

Dance the back, replace steps, facing the man in a basic hold. (Counts - quick, quick)

Continue with a Link.

CHANGE OF HANDS BEHIND THE BACK

This stylish figure is not at all difficult if the guidelines are followed. Start as usual when you have just danced the standard back, replace steps and are in an open position.

1 Man

Rock forward onto the left foot and place the woman's right hand into your right hand. (Count - slow)

Woman

Rock forward onto the right foot, aiming slightly towards your left of the man. (Count - slow)

Changing Hands

It is the man's job to change hands when required by the next figure. The Change of Place Right to Left and Left to Right can both be concluded with either of the man's hands. If a turn under the arm has taken place, you should complete the change of hands at the end of the downward arm movement. Never let go of the woman's hand until you have placed it into your other hand.

2 Man

Rock to the side onto the right foot, making a quarter turn to the left. Placing both hands behind your back, transfer the woman's right hand into your left hand. End with your back to the woman. (Count - slow)

Woman

Rock to the side onto the left foot, making a quarter turn to the right. End facing the man's back. (Count - slow)

3–4 Man

Dance the back, replace steps, making a quarter turn to the left to end facing the woman in an open position. (Counts - quick, quick)

Woman

Dance the back, replace steps, making a quarter turn to the right to end facing the man in an open position. (Counts - quick, quick)

Rock 'n' Roll Style

Now that you are familiar with some of the classic rock 'n' roll figures, you can concentrate on perfecting that rock 'n' roll style

Suggested Programme

1 Rock Basic
2 Throwaway
3 Underarm Turn to the Right
4 American Spin, ending in a right hand to right hand hold
5 Comb
6 Change of Hands behind the Back
7 Change of Place Left to Right
8 Double Spin, changing to a right hand to right hand hold and ending in an open position
9 Half Catapult
10 Jig Walks

• Generally keep the steps small. Remember that the objective is not to move around the floor.

• The man should avoid concentrating on what his partner is doing and should never follow her. Don't look at each other's feet. In many dances, when the woman steps backwards, the man steps forward. This is not the case in rock 'n' roll, so it is far better to concentrate on your own steps and moves.

• Don't under any circumstances fudge the moves. Be accurate and clear.

• Maintain a steady rhythm and stick to it. The man should not, for example, hesitate to allow extra time for the woman to complete a turn or spin.

• Don't be tempted to take short cuts. Women in particular must avoid turning too early. Learn the moves properly and you will quickly get them working for you instead of you working at them.

• Keep the movements compact. Avoid getting too far away from your partner, as this will make the dance uncomfortable and you may lose contact with each other.

LEADING

You will already have picked up many useful and practical tips on leading through dancing the figures you have learned so far. Here are some further points to help you.

• If the woman is turning in front of the man, both the man's and the woman's arm must be toned. The man leads the woman only by arm movements which are forward or backward in relation to his own hips, or by raising the arm.. This causes the woman to pivot on her own foot and make the turn. The man's arm should never be extended with a view to pulling or pushing the woman.

• In the open position, the man's hand should be palm uppermost with the woman's fingers held lightly between the man's palm and thumb.

• The man should always raise his arm high enough for the woman to turn beneath it comfortably, without having to duck.

• When the man leads the woman to turn or spin under his arm to the right using his right hand, the palm of the hand should first be rolled through 270° in the woman's hand until the two hands are again palm to palm. The back of the man's right hand will now be facing his body. If the right arm is now extended to a point above the woman's head and then lowered behind her head, she will automatically be led to turn. The man should decide how quickly to lower his arm in order to be in time with the rhythm of the music. The speed of lowering the arm has a direct effect on the speed of the woman's turn or spin.

Chicken Walks and Jump

Now it's time to have more fun with another figure that has withstood the test of time. The Chicken Walks originated with the Lindy Hop and were used throughout the Jitterbug years before becoming a favorite with Rock 'n' Rollers. The figure starts with an Overturned Throwaway.

OVERTURNED THROWAWAY

1–2 Man

Dance Steps 1 and 2 of the standard Throwaway. At the end of Step 2, firmly bring the left arm back a little to turn the woman to face you. (Counts - slow, slow)

1 Woman

Rock forward onto the right foot, toward the man's left side. (Count - slow)

2 Woman

Standing on the right foot, turn to face away from the man and rock forward onto the left foot into an open position. Do not fully extend your arm or take too big a step. Standing on the left foot, swivel to the right to face the man with knees together, the left knee flexed and the right knee extended straight forward with the right foot turned out a little. (Count - slow)

> You should now feel tension through the arms and as if you and your partner are pulling away from each other slightly.

CHICKEN WALKS

1 Man
Close the left foot to the right foot. (Count - slow)

Woman
Transfer your body weight forward onto the right foot. With knees together, point the left foot straight forward and turn it out slightly. (Count -slow)

2 Man
Take a small step backwards onto the right foot. (Count - slow)

Woman
Transfer your body weight forward onto the left foot. With knees together, point the right foot forward and turn it out slightly. (Count - slow)

Style Tip

The action of the Chicken Walks is very important in order to get the classic look and feel. While taking a step backwards with the right foot, the right toe is placed against the left heel. The heel is only lowered when you transfer your body weight to allow the left foot to move backwards on the next step. The same action is used when taking a step backwards onto the left foot.

3 Man

Take a small step backwards onto the left foot. (Count - quick)

3–6 Woman

Repeat Steps 1 and 2 twice. (Counts - quick, quick, quick, quick)

4 Man

Take a small step backwards onto the right foot. (Count - quick)

5–6 Man

Repeat Steps 3 and 4. (Counts - quick, quick)

JUMP

1 Man and Woman

Jump forward towards your partner, landing on both feet, with feet apart and knees very flexed. (Count - quick)

2 Man and Woman

Pause (Count - quick)

> Continue with a Rock Basic or Throwaway or another Overturned Throwaway leading into the Chicken Walks. The first rock to follow the Jump will simply be a transfer of your body weight as the foot is already in position. Now add the Chicken Walks from an Overturned Throwaway after the Jig Walks in your practice programme.

WHAT TO DO WITH THE FREE ARM

In open positions, one of your arms will be free. Generally, for the man, it should be held out to the side. This will help enormously with balance. The arm can also mimic the movement of the arm through which you are leading your partner, which will again help with balance. Above all, you should not feel inhibited about using the free arm but should make any moves with it natural. Avoid putting your free hand down by your side or, even worse, on your hip. Make your free arm work for you.

The woman should follow the same general guidelines as those given for the man. In addition, it is useful to know what to do with the free arm during turns. Generally, at the beginning of a turn or spin, bring the arm quickly across the body, which will assist the turn. As the turn or spin is completed, bring the free arm out to the side. This needs to be done early enough to avoid hitting the man.

37

Link and Whip

Most of the figures learned so far use the standard rhythm of "slow, slow, quick, quick". Exciting effects can be produced with simple figures using a different rhythm. Here is a good example of one such figure, also known as the Lindy Turn. It consists of a close hold turn to the right and, as you become familiar with the move, you will be able to whip it around. Start in an open position with the woman's right hand in the man's left. The man is standing of the right foot and the woman on the left after having danced the standard back, replace steps.

1 Man
Rock forward onto the left foot with the knee flexed, drawing the woman towards you into a close hold and starting to turn to the right.
(Count - slow)

Woman
Step forward onto the right foot, placing it between the man's feet and take up a close hold.
(Count - slow)

2 Man
Cross the right foot behind the left foot, turning the right toe and knee out and turning the body to the right in the Whip. (Count - quick)

Woman
Step to the side onto the left foot, turning to the right with the man.
(Count - quick)

3 Man

Step to the side onto the left foot, continuing to turn to the right.
(Count - quick)

Woman

Step onto the right foot, continuing to turn to the right with the man. Depending on the rate of turn generated by the man, the right foot may hardly move or you may take a small step forward and across. Point the right foot towards the man in order to keep your hips and shoulders parallel with his.
(Count - quick)

4 Man

Rock to the side onto the right foot.
(Count - slow)

Woman

Rock to the side onto the left foot.
(Count - slow)

5–6 Man

Dance the back, replace steps. (Counts - quick, quick)

Woman

Dance the back, replace steps. (Counts - quick, quick)

Continue with a Rock Basic, a Change of Place Right to Left, a Throwaway or another appropriate figure.

Throwaway Whip

An alternative version of the Link and Whip is the Throwaway Whip, where the woman moves away from the man after the Whip. This starts in the same way as the previous figure, with the man standing on the right foot, and the woman on the left, after having danced the back, replace steps.

1 Man

Rock forward onto the left foot with the knee flexed, drawing the woman towards you into a very close hold. (Count - slow)

Woman

Step forward onto the right foot, placing it between the man's feet and take up a close hold. (Count - slow)

2 Man

Cross the right foot behind the left foot, turning the right toe and knee out and turning the body to the right in the Whip. (Count - quick)

Woman

Step to the side onto the left foot, turning strongly to the right with the man. (Count - quick)

3 Man

Step to the side onto the left foot, continuing to turn to the right and releasing hold with the right hand and extending the left arm to lead the woman away from you. (Count - quick)

Woman

Step forward and across the left foot with the right foot, starting to move away from the man. (Count - quick)

4 Man

Rock back and to the side onto the right foot, ending in an open position. (Count - slow)

Woman

Rock back onto the left foot, ending in an open position. (Count - slow)

5–6 Man

Dance the back, replace steps. (Counts - quick, quick)

Woman

Dance the back, replace steps. (Counts - quick, quick)

Arm Breaker

This is the move that everyone wants to be able to do. In Jive, it is called the Apache Spin and, in the Lindy Hop, it is the Texas Tommy. In Rock 'n' Roll, the name of this advanced figure gives warning of the need to practise it slowly at first, while you gradually get used to the timing and feel of the move. When danced at full speed, the Arm Breaker is quite spectacular. Start in an open position with the woman's right hand in the man's left. Having just danced the standard back, replace steps, the man is standing on the right foot and the woman on the left foot. During the whole figure, you should make at least a half turn to the right.

1 Man
Rock forward onto the left foot, starting to turn to the right and leading the woman towards your right side. Then, still holding the woman's right hand in your left, place both hands behind her back at waist level. (Count - slow)

Woman
Rock forward onto the right foot, towards the man's right side. (Count - slow)

▼ **2 Man**

Cross the right foot behind the left foot, turning the right toe and knee out and continue turning to the right. Transfer the woman's right hand from your left hand into your right hand and start to pull downwards with your right hand, leading the woman to turn to the right. (Count - quick)

Woman

Take very small steps on Steps 2 and 3, so that you are dancing virtually on the spot. Standing on the right foot, turn to the right and step to the side onto the left foot, allowing the man to move your right arm behind your back. (Count - quick)

▲ **3 Man**

Step to the side onto the left foot, continuing to turn to the right and still pulling down with the right hand until the woman has "unwound". (Count - quick)

Woman

Continue to unwind and step onto the right foot. (Count - quick)

Continue with a triple step or chassé, which comprises three steps danced to two beats of music:

4 Man
Step to the side onto the right foot.
(Count - quick)
Woman
Step to the side onto the left foot.
(Count - quick)

MUSIC SUGGESTION

"Tutti Frutti" by Little Richard (Specialty Records) is a medium tempo number that picks up the pace.

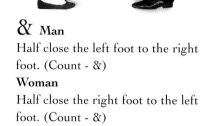

& Man
Half close the left foot to the right foot. (Count - &)
Woman
Half close the right foot to the left foot. (Count - &)

5 Man
Step to the side onto the right foot.
(Count - quick)
Woman
Step to the side onto the left foot.
(Count - quick)

6–7 Man
Dance the back, replace steps.
(Counts - quick, quick)
Woman
Dance the back, replace steps.
(Counts - quick, quick)

ARM BREAKER WITH TRIPLE SPIN

An even flashier, but more advanced finish is for the woman to dance a Triple Spin while the man dances the Triple Step or Chassé. Dance the figure as described previously, with the following modifications:

1–3 Dance up to Step 3 of the Arm Breaker. At the end of this step, the man will raise the right arm above the woman's head. (Counts - slow, quick, quick)

4 Man
Lower the right arm, leading the woman to spin a half turn (Count - quick)
Woman
Spin a half turn to end facing the man. (Count - quick)

The man must lead these moves correctly and not wait for the woman to complete the spins on her own. By raising and lowering his arm on the appropriate counts, he will assist the woman to turn in time.
The woman should allow the man to lead her to make three spins. Keep the feet apart and legs braced throughout

& Man
Raise the right arm, leading the woman to spin a further half turn. (Count - &)
Woman
Spin a half turn to end with your back to the man. (Count - &)

5 Man
Lower the right arm, leading the woman to spin a final half turn. (Count - quick)
Woman
Spin a final half turn to end facing the man and relax. (Count - quick)

6–7 Man
Dance the back, replace steps.
Woman
Dance the back, replace steps.

Wrap

S tart this popular figure as usual after the standard back, replace steps, with the man standing on the right foot and the woman on the left. The couple are in an open facing position and have taken up a double hand hold during the back, replace steps. At the end of the back, replace steps of the previous move, the man should lead the woman towards him and start to raise his left hand.

1 Man

Rock to the side onto the left foot, leading the woman to turn to her left under your left arm, ending in a side-by-side position with the woman on your right. Then lower the left hand over the woman's head to a position in front of her waist, retaining a right hand to right hand hold. This is the Wrap. (Count - slow)

Woman

Rock forward onto the right foot, making a half turn on this foot to the left under the man's arm and end in a side-by-side position with the man on your left. (Count - slow)

2 Man

Step forward onto the right foot, circling clockwise and retaining the Wrap hold. (Count - quick)

Woman

Step backwards onto the left foot, circling clockwise. (Count - quick)

3 Man

Step forward onto the left foot, circling clockwise and retaining the Wrap hold. (Count - quick)

Woman

Step backwards onto the right foot, circling clockwise. Then swivel to the right on the right foot to face the man. (Count - quick)

4 Man

Releasing the left hand, draw the woman's left hand down with your right hand and rock to the side onto the right foot, ending facing the woman who has now rolled off your arm. (Count - slow)

Woman

Rock to the side onto the left foot to face the man. (Count - slow)

5—6 Man and Woman

Dance the standard back, replace steps with the woman's left hand in the man's right hand. (Counts - quick, quick)

Style Tip

As the woman rolls off the man's arm she will be given the momentum to spin to face her partner.

Continue with the Toe-heel Swivels, which come next.

Toe-heel Swivels

Stay on the spot to dance this figure, while you perform some fancy footwork. Rhythm is one of the vital keys to success and, once mastered, will be amply rewarded by the impressiveness of the Toe-heel Swivels. Adopt a double hand hold during the back, replace steps of the preceding figure. Start in an open facing position, with the man standing on the right foot and the woman on the left foot. Both the man and woman dance the same steps in this figure.

To start
The man and woman face one another, with the man on the right foot, and the woman on the left. Steps are described here for the man. The dancers will mirror one another's movements, so if the man swivels to his right, the woman will swivel to her left. All counts are quick.

1 Standing on the right foot, swivel a quarter turn to the right. Point the left toes next to the right toes.

2 Standing on the right foot, swivel a quarter turn to the left. Flick the left foot forward.

Continue by repeating all six steps if you wish, then follow with the Rock Basic or the Throwaway, which is better.

Style Tip

Brace the arms and work through them to assist the turns. Hold the hands and arms still, focusing all the action on the feet and legs. An alternative timing of "quick, quick, slow" can be used to practise while building up speed towards the preferable "all-quick" timing.

To add highlight to this figure, repeat the six steps and, on the second Step 6, flex the knees and stamp down hard into the floor. Hold the position perfectly still for a count of four, then resume.

4 Standing on the left foot, swivel to the left. Point the right toes next to the left toes.

5 Standing on the left foot, swivel to the right. Flick the right foot forward.

6 Standing on the left foot, swivel to the left. Cross the right foot over the left foot.

3 Standing on the left foot, swivel to the right. Cross the left foot over the right foot.

Full Catapult

You know the half catapult; now let's look at the full catapult. As always, start having completed the standard back, replace steps. The man is standing on the right foot and the woman on the left foot in an open facing position and in a right hand to left hand hold. The woman has more steps than the man in this figure, but the overall timing is the same and the couple will synchronize again on the back, replace steps.

1 Man
Rock to the left onto the left foot. Raise the right arm, leading the woman to turn to her left. (Count - slow)

Woman
Rock forward onto the right foot, turning to the left under the man's raised arm. (Count - slow)

2 Man
Rock to the right onto the right foot. Lower the right arm as the woman moves behind into a tandem position. Take up a double hand hold, with the arms extended behind. (Count - slow)

Woman
Rock to the side onto the left foot, having completed a half turn to the left. Take up a double hand hold behind the man. (Count - slow)

◀ **3 Man**

Check the left foot forward with your arms extended behind in a double hand hold. (Count - quick)

Woman

Rock backwards onto the right foot, pulling gently on the man's arms. (Count - quick)

▶ **4 Man**

Transfer your body weight back onto the right foot. (Count - quick)

Woman

Transfer your body weight forward onto the left foot. (Count - quick)

◀ **5 Man**

Release hold with the right hand and lead the woman forward to your left side. Rock to the side onto the left foot. (Count - slow)

Woman

Rock forward onto the right foot, moving past the man's left side, starting to turn to the right and releasing hold with the right hand. (Count - slow)

6 Man

Lead the woman across in front of you and lead her in a clockwise spin before releasing hold. Rock to the side onto the right foot. (Count - slow)

Woman

Step onto the left foot, spinning to the right. (Count - quick)

Step onto the right foot, spinning strongly to the right. (Count - &)

7–8 Man

Dance the standard back, replace steps, resuming an appropriate hold in an open facing position after the woman's spin. (Counts - quick, quick)

7 Woman

Rock to the side onto the left foot to end facing the man. (Count - quick)

8–9 Woman

Dance the standard back, replace steps. (Counts - quick, quick)

Continue with the Link, which will bring you back into your practice programme.

Embellishing Basic Moves

There are a number of great but not so difficult moves that can be added to basic figures. These can make a basic figure look completely different and even a relative beginner can look like an expert. They are fun, too!

AMERICAN SPIN WITH CROSSED DOUBLE HOLD

This enhancement of the American Spin uses both hands and arms, so take up a crossed double hold during the back, replace steps of the preceding figure – the man's right hand is holding the woman's right hand and his left hand is holding her left hand with the left hands on top. When dancing a figure from a crossed double hold, it is vital to remember which hand is on top. The man is standing on the right foot and the woman on the left foot.

1 Man

Rock onto the left foot. Raise the left hand above head height, drawing the woman towards you. Move the right hand smartly across the body from right to left at waist height, then release hold with the right hand to lead the woman's American Spin. (Count - slow)

Woman

Rock forward onto the right foot, moving towards the man. The man will raise your left hand to initiate your spin to the right. Release hold with the right hand, which is at waist height. (Count - slow)

2 Man

Rock to the side onto the right foot, turning a little to the left to end halfway toward a side-by-side position, hip to hip…

Woman

Still standing on the right foot, spin just over a complete turn to the right to end almost in a side-by-side position with the man on your left…

Woman's Style Tip

The amount of turn on the spin is greater than for the usual American Spin. The fact that the man is bringing your left hand down over his head in step 1 will largely compensate for this, so you don't need to power the turn as much as you might think.

On Step 2, the man many adopt a "sitting" position by additional flexing of the knees. In this case, your body weight should be evenly distributed over both feet and your knees should flex to the same extent as the man's. If the "sitting" position is used, hold it for count of "slow."

Man's Style Tip

This figure requires a degree of style. Don't worry about the woman following your lead – just relax and stay cool. On Step 2, flex the knees in a "sitting" position to add style to the move, keeping your body weight evenly distributed over both feet. Hold this position for a count of "slow". You can emphasize the step to the side onto the right foot by stamping the foot, but don't overdo it.

2 (continued) Man

… Move the free right hand around the woman's waist to catch her. Bring the left hand down over your head to place the woman's left hand across the back of your neck. (Count - slow)

Woman

… Rock to the side onto the left foot. The man will have brought your left hand over his head and placed it behind his neck. Allow your free right arm to move out to the side with the elbow flexed to aid balance. (Count - slow)

3–4 Man and Woman

Dance the usual back, replace steps in a side-by-side position. (Counts - quick, quick)

There are a number of options for resuming your programme after the American Spin with Crossed Double Hold.

Option 1: Jig Walks

Dance the Jig Walks in a standard close hold.

1 Man

Rock to the side onto the left foot, turning to the right to face the woman. Close the right arm towards you and place the left hand around the woman's back to lead the move. (Count - slow)

Woman

Rock to the side onto the right foot, turning to the left to face the man. Prepare to move the right arm across the man's back but above his left arm. (Count - slow)

Option 2: Opening out Movements

This introduces a variation to the standard count.

2–3 Man

Continue turning to the right, releasing the right hand. Moving into a side-by-side position with the woman on your left, dance the back, replace steps but this time starting with the right foot. Flex the right arm and allow it to move naturally out to the side. (Counts - quick, quick)

Woman

Continue turning to the left, releasing the left hand. Moving into a side-by-side position with the man on your right, dance the back, replace steps but this time starting with the left foot and with the right arm across the man's back. Flex the right arm and allow it to move naturally out to the side. (Counts - quick, quick)

56

MUSIC SUGGESTION

"Let's Have a Party" by Wanda Jackson (Capitol Records). What a great idea, and what better music to party to!

4 Man

Rock to the side onto the right foot, turning to the left to face the woman. Close the left arm towards you and place the right hand around the woman's waist to lead the move. (Count - slow)

Woman

Rock to the side onto the left foot, turning to the right to face the man. Prepare to move the left arm across the man's back but above his right arm. (Count - slow)

5–6 Man

Continue turning to the left, releasing the left hand. Moving into a side-by-side position with the woman on your right, dance the standard back, replace steps. (Counts - quick, quick)

Woman

Continue turning to the right, releasing the right hand. Moving into a side-by-side position with the man on your left, dance the standard back, replace steps with the left arm across the man's back and the right arm out to the side. (Counts - quick, quick)

Option 3: Change of Place Right to Left

Dance this figure as described earlier in the book. As in Option 2, dance the back, replace steps with the man drawing the woman to him on the rock. He then continues by taking the woman's right hand in his left hand and leading her to turn to the right for the Change of Place. He may gently push against the woman's back with the right hand to encourage and confirm the turn.

Combining the Options

The Jig Walks can be followed by the Opening out Movements and/or the Change of Place Right to Left.

This figure can now be repeated.

More Turns

In Rock 'n' Roll, your repertoire of turns can be dynamically increased using some simple modifications. So far, you have learned mainly underarm turns, as the simple action of the man raising his arm will naturally lead the woman to turn under it. There are also some very easy turns that do not require the woman to turn under the man's arm. Try the Change of Place Right to Left and the Change of Place Left to Right using a lead like that of the American Spin and releasing hold, so that the woman turns without going under the man's arm. The man can also make his own turns without going under the arm.

TURN TO THE LEFT FOR THE MAN

Start in an open facing position, with the woman's right hand in the man's left hand, having just danced the standard back, replace steps.

1 Man
Rock forward onto the left foot towards the woman.
(Count - slow)
Woman
Rock forward onto the right foot towards the man.
(Count - slow)

2 Man
Standing on the left foot, make about a quarter turn to the left and rock to the side onto the right foot to end with your back to the woman. Allow the left hand and arm to move across your waist. Move the right hand forward over the joined hands, then release hold with the left hand. (Count - slow)
Woman
Standing on the right foot, make about a quarter turn to the right and rock to the side onto the left foot to end facing the man's back. Release hold with the right hand. (Count - slow)

3–4 Man

Dance the back, replace steps, continuing to turn to the left to end facing the woman. Resume hold with the left hand. (Counts - quick, quick)

Woman

Dance the back, replace steps, continuing to turn to the right to end facing the man. Resume hold with the right hand. (Counts - quick, quick)

HALF PRETZEL

Here is another turn for the woman in which she dances under the man's arm. Take up a double hand hold

during the preceding back, replace steps in an open facing position. As additional confirmation of the lead

into the Half Pretzel, the man may incline the woman's left hand downwards on the second step of the back,

replace steps.

1 Man

Rock to the side onto the left foot. Raise the left arm to start leading the woman to turn to the right. (Count - slow)

Woman

Rock forward onto the right foot, starting to turn to the right underneath the man's left arm. (Count - slow)

2 Man

Rock to the side onto the right foot, starting to make a quarter turn to the left, with the left arm still raised. Turn the woman's left hand behind her back as she turns. (Count - slow)

Woman

Continue to turn to the right to complete a three-quarter turn underneath the man's left arm, allowing your left arm to turn into a position behind your back. (Count - slow)

3–4 Man

Dance the back, replace steps. (Counts - quick, quick)

Woman

Dance the back, replace steps facing the man. (Counts - quick, quick)

5 Man

Rock to the side onto the left foot, turning to the right. With the left arm still raised, lead the woman to turn by gently pulling down with the right hand. (Count - slow)

Woman

Rock to the side onto the right foot, making a quarter turn to the left to end with your back to the man. (Count - slow)

Variation

You can dance an alternative ending to the Half Pretzel which includes a turn for the man on Steps 5 and 6 by making the following modifications:

5 Man

Rock forward onto the left foot, moving underneath your left arm and releasing hold with the right hand. (Count - slow)

Woman

Rock forward onto the right foot, starting to turn to the right and releasing hold with the left hand. (Count - slow)

6 Man

Standing on the left foot, turn to the left and rock onto the right foot to end facing the woman. (Count - slow)

Woman

Rock to the side onto the left foot, completing the turn to the right to end facing the man. (Count - slow)

Finish with the usual back, replace steps
A good combination is to dance the
Half Pretzel twice. Then dance it a
third time, finishing with the
man's turn to the left.

6 Man

Rock to the side onto the right foot, facing the woman. (Count -slow)

Woman

Continue to turn to the left and rock to the side onto the left foot, ending facing the man. (Count -slow)

PRETZEL

When you have practised the Half Pretzel, you will probably want to try the complete Pretzel. This is more difficult but well worth the effort and practice. Dance up to and including Step 4 of the Half Pretzel. The man will now lead the woman to dance a spin across him before catching her in his right arm.

& Man
Half close the right foot to the left foot.
Woman
Step to the side onto the left foot, turning to the left to face the man.

2 Man
Step to the side onto the left foot. Lead the woman by pulling gently with the right hand to start her turn, then raise the right hand and lower the left hand to lead her to across in front of you. End facing the woman, holding her right hand behind her back. (Counts - quick, &, quick)
Woman
Step to the side onto the right foot, turning to the left to first back and then face the man. (Counts - quick, &, quick)

1 Man
Making almost a half turn to the right, dance a jive chassé: step to the side onto the left foot.
Woman
Step to the side onto the right foot, turning to the left to back the man.

Style Tip

The man should take care when leading the woman's spin, only raising the hand after the turn has started. For the woman all the steps should be small as you spin across the man in an anticlockwise direction.

We hope that you have enjoyed learning to dance some of the classic figures of rock 'n' roll contained in this book. Don't expect too much of yourself too soon. Take the time to learn the moves properly and you will feel more relaxed and confident when you dance them. Practice not only makes perfect, it makes possible.

3 Man

Dance the back step, starting with the right foot. (Count - quick).

Woman

Dance the back step, starting with the left foot. (Count - quick)

4 Man

Dance the replace step. (Count - quick)

Woman

Dance the replace step. (Count - quick)

Further Information

Why not get in touch with your local dance school or
Rock 'n' Roll club? Sharing and contributing to the pleasure of
others as you all learn to Rock 'n' Roll is not only much more
rewarding, it's so much more fun for everyone, including you.

Consult the yellow pages for dance schools in your area, or
look in your local listings magazines for information on
clubs and special events.

Acknowledgements
The author and publishers would like to thank the following for their
participation in the photography of this book. Their dance skills and
enthusiasm were invaluable.
Mark Feld, Natascha Hall, Tanya Janes, Helia Lloyd, Simon Selmon,
Eric Sille and Debbie Smith.

Author's Acknowledgements
I would like to thank Simon Selmon for his expertise and advice and also
Simon's friends and colleagues from the London Swing Dance Society.
Thanks also to Derek Young, whose enthusiasm for dancing in general
and Rock 'n' Roll in particular has always been inspirational and whose
book *Rock 'n' Roll Dancing* provided a valuable insight into many aspects of
the dance. Particular thanks must be reserved for my wife, Elaine, who
took over my teaching workload and provided much encouragement and
support throughout the preparation of this book.
Thanks 'Laine, for everything.

Picture Credits
The publishers would like to thank Super Stock for use of
the image on page 8.

Publisher's Note
Dancing is great fun and an excellent form of exercise but beginners
should take care to start off gently, and work their way up to more
advanced moves.